Little Laureates

Poems From Northern England Vol II

Edited by Heather Killingray

Young Writers
First published in Great Britain in 2007 by:
Young Writers
Remus House
Coltsfoot Drive
Peterborough
PE2 9JX
Telephone: 01733 890066
Website: www.youngwriters.co.uk

SB ISBN 978-1 84431 251 1

Foreword

Young Writers was established in 1991 and has been passionately devoted to the promotion of reading and writing in children and young adults ever since. The quest continues today. Young Writers remains as committed to the nurturing of poetic and literary talent as ever.

This year's Young Writers competition has proven as vibrant and dynamic as ever and we are delighted to present a showcase of the best poetry from across the UK and in some cases overseas. Each poem has been selected from a wealth of *Little Laureates* entries before ultimately being published in this, our sixteenth primary school poetry series.

Once again, we have been supremely impressed by the overall quality of the entries we have received. The imagination, energy and creativity which has gone into each young writer's entry made choosing the poems a challenging and often difficult but ultimately hugely rewarding task - the general high standard of the work submitted ensured this opportunity to bring their poetry to a larger appreciative audience.

We sincerely hope you are pleased with this final collection and that you will enjoy *Little Laureates Poems From Northern England Vol II* for many years to come.

Contents

The Poems

Viva Le Lance!

A whole year's worth of time and effort,
Enduring through suffering and pain,
Through blazing heat and searing winds,
Taking its toll.

All this training just for three weeks of cycling,
'Not worth it,' you say,
But all the training eventually pays off,
For Lance Armstrong.

Yet winning a race wasn't his greatest achievement
But beating cancer,
And the snarling jaws of death,
He did what was believed impossible.

Lance agonisingly fell from his bike,
Indescribable pain draining his energy and soul,
Rushed into hospital only to find he had cancer.
Lance's friends and family almost gave up all hope.

But not Lance . . .
Loved ones shedding tears of sorrow together but not Lance . . .
Doctors worried that chemotherapy wouldn't heal him,
But Lance didn't worry in the slightest . . .

Through sheer will and determination, Lance battled.
The eye of the storm of cancer was upon him,
But Lance didn't give up hope, not now.
Not the next day, not ever.

Lance barely survived a life-threatening illness . . .
Yet his will to live strong overthrew the disease.
Now he wears the ubiquitous yellow band . . .
Not as a coward but as a hero . . .
Seven times over.

A true legend . . .
Viva la Lance!

Matthew Gosling (11)

Kindness

Kindness is blue.
Kindness smells sweet.
Kindness tastes like fudge.
Kindness sounds like a flute.
Kindness makes you feel strong.

Camilla Robinson (10)
Allendale Middle School, Hexham

Changes

I sit and watch the sun come up,
I think about the life I've led.
I think I was good to my family,
Although I never wanted to go to bed.

I sit and watch the sun shine down,
From upon the midday sky.
I think about my childhood, my good times and my bad,
And how my mother used to say, 'You must always try.'

I sit and watch the sun go away,
I wonder what I did wrong.
Why am I here alone?
While the robin still chirrups his song.

I sit and watch the stars shine bright,
I wonder time and time again.
What has happened? Why am I on my deathbed,
In sickness and in pain?

From the heavens, the moon glares down
And now I realise
My message in life was not to triumph
But to know the world as it is now and
Be here while the wind still sighs.

Chloe Spurgeon (10)
Allendale Middle School, Hexham

Lion Heartbeat

My heart in my mouth,
As he approaches me,
His large velvet paws padding.
Amber eyes, bright and gleaming,
Like tiny lanterns in his head.

He stretches and crouches low,
Slinking straight at me and suddenly,
He pounces.

Ruby Parkinson (10)
Allendale Middle School, Hexham

Trees

Trees are spiritual
They bring out the good in people
Old or young, they are magic
The older the wiser
They help us breathe life
Trees have mysterious souls . . .
And always will have.
Trees will live on forever.

Kizzie Nicholson (11)
Allendale Middle School, Hexham

HBUAFC Poem

Red is the colour,
Football is our game,
We're all together
And winning is our aim.
So cheer us on through the sun and rain,
'Cause Haydon Bridge is our name.

Haydon Bridge
Haydon Bridge!

Brendon Conner Pearson (10)
Allendale Middle School, Hexham

The Buddha

This place is peaceful
This place is far away

I am looking at a carving
I am looking at a spirit in wood

I am thinking about trees and mountains
I am thinking about peace and harmony

I wonder if I can go there
I wonder about gold and silver

I am a relic
I am a Buddha.

Angus Lill (12)
Allendale Middle School, Hexham

The Tempest - Haiku

A storm, a shipwreck
Love, adventure, mystery
At last, forgiven!

Elliott Wallis (11)
Allendale Middle School, Hexham

Love!

Love is like a sweet red rose
Love has a button nose
Love is cute every day
Love can be expressed in different ways.
Love is love and I am me and my
Love is as good as can be
So hear me out as I say
Love can be everything you hear and say.

Katie Alderson (9)
Allendale Middle School, Hexham

My Forest, Found Poem

This place is peaceful
This place is quiet
This place is darkness mixed with sunlight
Created an atmosphere unimaginable.

I wonder how this place came to be
I wonder how trees came to stand where they stand
I wonder how the river came to flow.

I am thinking of the future, will this place still be here?
I am thinking of the past, what was it like?
I am thinking, I am thinking.

I am in this place surrounded by nature
I am in amongst the trees, listening.

I am looking at a forest, peaceful, quiet
I am looking at a stream, gently trickling
I am looking, I am looking.

Laura Goodfellow (12)
Allendale Middle School, Hexham

The Frog

Jump about all day
Hip, hop, hip, hop
Splish, splash, splosh
Look there he goes *plop!*

Corinne Deal (10)
Crosby-on-Eden CE Primary School, Carlisle

Blackbird - Haiku

Gazing in the field
I saw a biggish blackbird
Sitting on a fence.

Anna Fisher (10)
Crosby-on-Eden CE Primary School, Carlisle

My Excitement

My excitement is yummy
It tastes like a sugary sweet
It smells of jelly beans
It sounds funny
It's tingly and jumpy
Just like a bunny.

My excitement.

Jemima Elgey (10)
Crosby-on-Eden CE Primary School, Carlisle

Great Goalkeeper - Cinquain

I play
football with friends
I am a goalkeeper
I save all of the penalties
Safe hands.

Kevin McKenna (10)
Crosby-on-Eden CE Primary School, Carlisle

Carlisle - Cinquain

Carlisle
are fantastic
I watch them every week
from the family stand, I shout
'Go Blues!'

Jack Little (9)
Crosby-on-Eden CE Primary School, Carlisle

A Joyful June - Cinquain

Hot June
Makes ice creams melt
Skin turned brown, hosepipe ban
June is a good time to sunbathe
Hooray!

Emma Hinde (9)
Crosby-on-Eden CE Primary School, Carlisle

The Life Of A Slave

The slaves arrived and immediately
Started work on the plantations,
Ready for the cotton to be taken,
To the other nations.

They worked and worked all day long,
And got whipped,
Though they did nothing wrong.

The slaves were starving
And treated badly,
The owners didn't care,
That most of them died, very sadly.

Slavery was abolished in 1807
But that was no use, it just
Stopped the ships coming from Devon.

Many years later the
Slaves were set free
And finally they were allowed
To go back across the sea.

Millie Phillips (10)
Crosby-on-Eden CE Primary School, Carlisle

Chloraphobia

I'm scared of clowns
I have no idea why
But whenever they come near me
I suddenly start to cry.

I need to sort this problem out
I've done it since I was 11
It's really, really bugging me
'Cause now I'm 37.

They call this chloraphobia
Well that's what I've been told
So I'm going to a therapist
Before I get too old.

Rebecca Irwin (11)
Crosby-on-Eden CE Primary School, Carlisle

My Dream

Galloping along,
With the wind in my hair,
Not a single thing in my mind,
But my beautiful mare.
Jumping over hedges
And soaring over tiny streams.
This has got to be my number one dream.

Sarah Jordan (11)
Crosby-on-Eden CE Primary School, Carlisle

Arachnaphobia

I am scared of all spiders,
Like a jumper is afraid of an iron,
Like a zebra is scared of a lion,
Like meat is terrified of a knife,
Like death is horrified of life,
Like a pig's afraid of slaughter,
Like a father's scared of his daughter.
I am scared of all spiders.

Taya Dixon (11)
Crosby-on-Eden CE Primary School, Carlisle

I Play Football - Cinquain

I play
football at parks
I score top corner kicks
They are the best goals I can do
oh yes!

Jamie Blake (9)
Crosby-on-Eden CE Primary School, Carlisle

Rugby Rules

I love rugby
like people being mad about motorbikes
like squirrels loving nuts
like cooks loving cooking
I love rugby.

Harvey Woodmass (9)
Crosby-on-Eden CE Primary School, Carlisle

Liverpool - Cinquain

The Reds
Best ever team
Anfield is where they play
The Champions League Final here
We come!

Jack Dixon (10)
Crosby-on-Eden CE Primary School, Carlisle

The Weather

The sun and the sky, what a wonderful tie,
The air so sweet, so soft and neat.

The snow and the rain down every street
Lots of happy people, I would be glad to meet.

The weathers of the world,
A snowball hurled.
The love and the life, the sun's poor strife
This is why I love the weather.

Ashley Hinson (9)
Crosby-on-Eden CE Primary School, Carlisle

Feelings

Happiness is yellow, like the hot burning sun,
It tastes like ice lollies on a warm summer's day.
It smells like freshly cut grass,
It looks like a team who have just won,
It sounds like young children having fun.

Sadness is deathly red like pure blood,
It tastes like bitter grapefruit,
It smells like a roaring fire,
It looks like a dead body, certainly not good,
It sounds like a chainsaw cutting wood.

Nervousness is green like a person who's ill,
It tastes like a sour lemon,
It smells like fear,
It looks as if it's about to kill.
It sounds like an old bicycle falling down a hill.

Scaredness is black like the evening sky,
It tastes like blood running down my throat.
It smells like burnt sausages,
it looks like flames, so tall, they are sky high,
It sounds like a child screeching. My oh my!

Alice Calvert (11)
Crosby-on-Eden CE Primary School, Carlisle

Newcastle United

The Newcastle United football team 2007
(1) is Shay Given the Irish goalkeeper,
(2) is Stephen Carr in the defence
(3) is Solano the right winger from Peru
(4) is Kieron Dyer the centre midfield
(5) is Martins the super scorer
(6) is Owen the England star
(16) is Milner the skilful winger
(17) is Parker the Newcastle captain
(19) is Bramble the rock in defence
(27) is Taylor the local defender
(33) is Babayaro the left back
This the Newcastle football team.

Jack Thorpe (11)
Crosby-on-Eden CE Primary School, Carlisle

Slavery Began

Slavery began long ago,
Lots of people were taken
From their African homes.

They were taken from their families,
Without any warning.
All they were fed were beans.

On the ship they were cramped,
They were stuck there for months,
They could barely move, they were just slumped.

A six month journey around the lands,
They were taken away,
From their home, with the sand.

Alice McDonald (11)
Crosby-on-Eden CE Primary School, Carlisle

On The Pirate Ship

On the pirate ship there are lots of different things.
An awesome, azure, acrobat a-bounding.
A brilliant, blue, brush basking.
A crazy, crimson, cockroach cackling.
A dim-witted, dark dog drooling.
An evil, emerald, exoskeleton eyeing.
A foolish flame Frankenstein fiddling.
A gargantuan green germ giggling.
A happy hazel hamster haggling.
An inter-admirable indigo Indiana Jones investigating.
A juicy jade juggler jumping.
A know-it-all khaki kangaroo kick-boxing.
A lucky lime llama launching.
A macabre maroon macaroni magnetising.
A natural navy narrator nibbling.
An optimistic orange orang-utan organising.
A pale pink parallelogram paralysing.
A queasy quicksilver quadrant quivering.
A ragged red raven rationalising.
A seasonal scarlet schoolchild synergising.
A tactical tartan teddy bear taxing.
An untruthful umber usurper upholding.
A vacant violet vegetable vibrating.
A wishful white watchdog waltzing.
An exciting xantic xylophone x-raying.
A youthful yellow yoga yelping.
A zealous zeal zealot zigzagging
On the pirate ship.

James Whitehead (11)
Crosby-on-Eden CE Primary School, Carlisle

Football

Football is fabulous, football is phenomenal,
The bounce of the ball, the roar of the crowd.
England, France, Germany, Spain they all have a League.
The world cup is the best,
England versus Brazil, France versus Italy
But no matter who wins I'll always say football is phenomenal.

Ryan Hogg (10)
Guide Post Middle School, Choppington

Chocolate

Chocolate is brown, white and delicious,
It melts in your mouth when you
shove it in.
It looks like you want to dive
right in it.
Chocolate reminds me of happiness.

Bethaney Roughead (10)
Guide Post Middle School, Choppington

Hate

Hate is black like a panther,
Hate is like a rat.
Hate is like a pan getting hotter.
Hate is like a lion getting angry.

Lewis Cockburn (9)
Guide Post Middle School, Choppington

Woof

I am a dog
But I am always soggy
With the fur in my eyes, it gets very foggy,
I always play with my ball,
Running down the hall.
Woof! Woof! I get very dizzy
As I play with my friend Muzzie.
I hope I don't chase a cat
Because I am wearing a hat.

Oops!

Jessica Dawson (10)
Guide Post Middle School, Choppington

Anger

Anger feels like a kettle steaming inside me,
It looks like a bull charging in a frenzy.
Anger smells like molten lava bubbling hot and fresh.
It tastes bitter and burnt like the inside of a dirty oven.
Anger sounds like World War II.
The colour of anger is red, orange and yellow
As it gets you in its grasp.
Anger reminds me of a meteorite shooting through Earth.

Kiana Leonard (10)
Guide Post Middle School, Choppington

Fun

Fun tastes like sweets and sugar, when you're feeling happy,
Fun looks like a big joyful dolphin, twirling away.
Fun sounds like a crowd, screeching for the match on a special day.
Fun reminds me of whizzing down the road on my brand new bike.
Fun feels like a jump into a swimming pool on a sunny day,
Fun smells of chocolate cake for a fresh start,
Fun's colour is yellow for a big bright sun.
To lead you on your way.

Molly Sale (9)
Guide Post Middle School, Choppington

Laughter

Laughter is orange like the sun setting below the horizon.
Laughter feels like a rainbow creating inside you.
Laughter sounds like a beautiful choir inside your voice box.
Laughter looks like little bouncing clowns jumping in front of you.
Laughter reminds me of when all the family get together and have a good time.
Laughter tastes of delicious foods trickling down your throat.
Laughter smells of hot chocolate wafting under your nose.
Laughter makes your day!

Sarah Squires (10)
Guide Post Middle School, Choppington

Fun

Fun is mulitcoloured like a rainbow shining brightly in the sky.
Fun feels like flowers and cuddly toys.
Fun looks like roses all over the floor.
Fun sounds like trees blowing in the wind.
Fun smells like fudge and caramel.
Fun tastes like strawberries and everything sweet.
Fun reminds me of laughter and happiness.

Charlotte Ford (10)
Guide Post Middle School, Choppington

Fun

Fun feels like when you know you did something right.
Fun looks like baby animals in the spring.
Fun is the colour of gold, silver and green.
Fun tastes like chocolate and sweets.
Fun sounds like children playing on a weekend.
Fun smells like toffee being made.
Fun reminds me of chocolate ice cream and anything sweet.

Emily Jones (10)
Guide Post Middle School, Choppington

Fear

Fear tastes like a raw eagle.
Fear feels like a van running you down.
Fear looks like a gunshot.
Fear smells like a burned out car.
Fear reminds me of a murderer.
Fear is red and orange like the colour of fire.
Fear sounds like a bomb being set off.

Callum Muckle (9)
Guide Post Middle School, Choppington

Laughter

Laughter sounds like a bubbling brook.
Laughter tastes like fresh apples.
Laughter feels like fluffy clouds.
Laughter looks like a big rainbow smiling at you.
Laughter is orange like a sunset over the hills.
Laughter reminds me of my family and friends.
Laughter smells like a sweet perfume spreading over the room.

Melissa James (10)
Guide Post Middle School, Choppington

Hate

It sounds like anger,
Bulldozers knocking down buildings,
People going crazy.
It feels like you want to attack someone
Or you want to run away.
It tastes like burning coal,
Rocks and burnt toast.
It's red and orange and dark, very dark.
It looks like World War II
And an erupting volcano.
It reminds me of wars and anger
And the London bombings.
It smells of burning and blood and rotten fish.

Nathan Ho (9)
Guide Post Middle School, Choppington

Footy

Footy looks like the best thing in the world to me.
When you step in the stadium you can't believe the atmosphere.
Loads of people going mad over one thing,
Football, the best game in the world.
This is our thing,
This is our element,
This is our game,
This is our season.

Matthew Dunn (10)
Guide Post Middle School, Choppington

Fun

Fun has the colour of pink, red and all light colours.
Fun feels like sharing and happiness.
Fun tastes like candy and chocolate.
Fun smells like flowers and roses.
Fun sounds like laughter of children.
Fun looks like happiness.
Fun feels like pleasure and goodness.
Fun reminds me of the fair.

Bronwyn Monaghan (9)
Guide Post Middle School, Choppington

Happiness

Happiness is yellow, red, dark orange and warm colours,
It feels like my favourite teddy bear, all soft and cuddly.
It looks like a warm and welcoming home, and your biggest smile.
Happiness sounds like walking into a fair and listening
To all the giggles and laughter of the children.
It smells like candyfloss and toffee apples.
Happiness tastes like the popcorn you get at the cinema.
Happiness reminds me of Disneyland.

Sarah Houlis (10)
Guide Post Middle School, Choppington

Fear

Fear looks like the haunted house across the road,
It makes you feel shivery and shaky.
Fear is black like the darkness of the midnight sky,
It tastes like a dry tablet waiting to make you ill.
Fear sounds like the queer sound of a girl screaming,
It reminds me of dead bodies waiting to haunt me.

Ashleigh Watson (10)
Guide Post Middle School, Choppington

Bradley Norris

My name is Bradley Norris
And I hate eating porridge.

I like sticky toffee
But I hate it really sloppy,

Especially with lots of toffee.

Bradley Norris (10)
Guide Post Middle School, Choppington

Monkeys

Monkeys are my favourite animal,
They are small and fluffy and funny too.
I remember monkeys from their
Swinging from tree to tree.
Orang-utans are so funny,
I will never forget them, no matter what.
I like monkeys because I am one!

Matthew Ord (10)
Guide Post Middle School, Choppington

Death

Death is a man made out of cloak and bones.
Death comes to you when you die, to take your soul.
He does not believe in mercy.
He does nothing to stop you dying.
People who don't believe in him,
They are the first to die.
So Death is a skeleton with a scythe
And people who fear him, he likes the most.

Evan Drysdale (9)
Guide Post Middle School, Choppington

Dolphins

Dolphins dive, dolphins glide,
Twirling and twisting throughout the sea.
Inviting their dolphin friends home for tea,
Eating seaweed,
Eating plants while they dance and prance.
They play throughout the day,
Now it's time to swim home and sleep,
Sleep tight, little dolphins.
Goodnight.

Natasha Gallon (9)
Guide Post Middle School, Choppington

Laughter

Laughter is like a yellow sunshine.
Laughter sounds like high notes on a piano.
Laughter feels like a tickle in your throat.
Laughter smells like bowls of fruit.
Laughter looks like snow falling heavily.
Laughter reminds me of playing in the snow.
Laughter tastes like a big juicy melon.
Laughter is made by your friends and family.
Laughter sometimes brings friendship together.

Billy Bryson (10)
Guide Post Middle School, Choppington

Horse

They trot very rough,
and some are tough.
When you ride,
you will get a suprise.
If you buy,
you will not sigh.
When you look at them in the eye,
they will look as if they're saying, 'Hi'.
Believe me you will,
I've been through all of this!

Stephanie Barrett (10)
Guide Post Middle School, Choppington

Animals

Dogs like bones,
Rabbits like carrots,
Birds like seeds,
Giraffes like weeds,
Monkeys like bananas,
Horses eat hay,
Mice eat cheese,
Cats eat grains
And humans eat everything!

Sophie Anderson (10)
Guide Post Middle School, Choppington

Ice Skating

Ice skating is a fun sport,
It always makes you smile,
Even when you fall over,
Everyone will always laugh.
When you're down you can just say,
'Can we go ice skating today?'

Faye Sanderson (9)
Guide Post Middle School, Choppington

Friends

Friends are kind,
They help you when you're down.
Friends keep a secret
If you tell them one.
They always come
To your birthday party.
Friends come and seek you
And walk to school with you.
Friends make me feel like
I've won a football cup.

Andrew Alexander (9)
Guide Post Middle School, Choppington

Kennings

It's a . . .
Fish cruncher,
Man muncher,
Clam smasher,
Water dasher,
Tail flapper,
Mischief maker,
It's a . . .

Jonathan Appleby (10)
Guide Post Middle School, Choppington

Dolphins

Dolphins are swift like a cheetah,
Dolphins are faster than me,
Dolphin calls give me headaches,
Dolphins are mammals like us,
Dolphins are cleverer than the teacher,
I love dolphins!

Adam Shepherd (9)
Guide Post Middle School, Choppington

Fear

Fear is like meeting an undertaker.
Fear is blood leaking from a cauldron.
Fear is like meeting the Great Khali in a dark alley.
Fear is dark and freaky.
Fear is like getting kidnapped.
Fear is like being sick.
Fear is like a vampire sucking blood.

Jason Wilshaw (9)
Guide Post Middle School, Choppington

Golf

Golf is a friendly and patient game.
It is all about co-ordination.
Golf is all fun and going on holiday
And like having a birthday.

Conor Turnbull (9)
Guide Post Middle School, Choppington

Happiness

Happiness is a colour like a yellowy-orange bubbling up.
Happiness tastes like a sweet and juicy apple.
Happiness reminds me of smiles everywhere.
Happiness looks like a chocolate bar walking through the door.
Happiness cheers everybody up when they're down.
I am happy when I am playing out with my friends.
I was happy when my mam got back with her old friend.

Chloe Ellison (10)
Guide Post Middle School, Choppington

What Am I?

I can run but can't walk,
I have a bottom but can't sit,
I'm see-through,
I'm a live thing that can't be held.
What am I?

A: A river.

Tilli Saunders (9)
Guide Post Middle School, Choppington

Fear

Fear is black like the undertaker's cape.
Fear is like the bogeyman's hand on your shoulder.
Fear is like a skeleton's hand rising from the ground.
Fear is like a thousand rotten fish on a windy beach.
Fear is like 500 cockroaches in a junkyard.
Fear is like a terrifying scream from the bathroom.

Gage Gallagher (9)
Guide Post Middle School, Choppington

Footy

Football is the best thing I want to do.
Football is like a good game to play.
Football has rules and a ref.
Football, it's a good job to get.
Football has a season
And football's got a league table
And teams to battle with.

Joe Reid (10)
Guide Post Middle School, Choppington

Football

Football is exciting,
It helps you exercise.
It reminds me of Ronaldinho,
It's my favourite sport.
It's exciting when you score.
My favourite player is Rooney.
It helps you to keep fit.

Ryan Young (10)
Guide Post Middle School, Choppington

Darkness

Darkness is pitch-black and blue,
The sky is only lit by moonlight
And the street is only lit by street lights.
Darkness is dull and gloomy,
It makes the atmosphere full of sadness
And horrible dreams floating around.
It reminds me of horror movies,
When people and phantoms creep
And sneak around in the dark.
It also reminds me of Hallowe'en,
When people are dressed up as witches,
Vampires, ghosts and pumpkins.
Darkness sounds like wolves howling in the distance
And waking you up all the time.
It smells like rotting flesh with blood
Running out of it and leaving a trail all over.
Darkness tastes like burning food
Which is making smoke float all through the house.

Lauren Gray (10)
Guide Post Middle School, Choppington

Happiness

Happiness tastes like hot roasting turkey
Happiness feels like a cosy bed,
Happiness looks like a teddy bear.
Happiness smells like flowers.
Happiness reminds me of Christmas,
Happiness is the colour of the golden sun.
Happiness sounds like people laughing their heads off.

Liam Dodds (9)
Guide Post Middle School, Choppington

Little Fishes

Fishes swim about wondering what to do,
Beware of sharks they can do things too
Sharks are big, fish and small,
But sharks aren't as greedy for fish, but catfish!
The only good things for catfish is that dogfish
Never existed.

Tom Smith (9)
Guide Post Middle School, Choppington

Sunflower

S izzling colours
U nusual
N utritious
F antastic
L ovely
O ily
W ithering
E xciting
R ound kite.

Shanine Summers (9)
Hipsburn First School, Alnwick

Sunflower

Sunflower seed growing, wind blowing,
Morning has come, the day has just begun.
Seed approaching, the seed is growing,
Blossoming sizzling colours.

Sunlight, raindrops, raindrops, sunlight,
Blossoming more, growing more,
Pushing bigger than ever,
Too much, drenched, dying,
Seeds passing, reducing.

Kathryn Spink (8)
Hipsburn First School, Alnwick

Who Am I?

My roots burst through my hard, cold pod,
And my head saw the light.
Never before had I received such a fright.

Chorus:
I'm taller than any daisy,
I'm taller than any leaf,
I'm taller than plant or bush
I'm really a tree.

My petals are coloured crimson,
My stalk is coloured green.

Edward Brunton (9)
Hipsburn First School, Alnwick

Sunlight

I must break out so I can feast on the dazzling sunlight,
I must grow higher and higher so I can blow in the wind.
I must stay tall and high, so I can drink the sweet, salty rain.

Jonathan Trapp (9)
Hipsburn First School, Alnwick

From Beginning To End

And the long journey begins as a tiny seed grows up, up, up,
gently and in slow motion.

It needs to get out, it needs to see sight of the sun.
'I'm getting out. I'm coming.'

A tiny stick, a green stalk, the flower had sprouted.
Next, a spiky leg, a pink firing flower, a little beautiful bush.

But oh no! The scariest noise, a gardener.
We knew.
So we quietly slept and never woke again.

Kelly Chowdhury (8)
Hipsburn First School, Alnwick

My Way Out!

Where am I? First I was in the blazing hot, fiery sun
but now I'm in a moist dark place.

Let me out, I want to get out!
Then the moist place was getting more and more moist.
I'm going to drown!

Soon I was starting to sprout down.
Help! I'm going to sizzle.
But then to the rescue, the water was back.

Jennifer Kay (8)
Hipsburn First School, Alnwick

My Flower Poem

A seed was planted
The roots grew
The little green shoots pushed their way out of the soil,
The stem reached out for the clear blue sky.

The leaves, as green as fresh grass grew onto the stem.
The golden petals, as yellow as the sun grew onto the new flower.

But what's this?
Summer has gone,
Autumn has come.
So cold!
The lovely flower suddenly fell asleep
And never woke again!

Sarah Spink (9)
Hipsburn First School, Alnwick

Invisible

If I were invisible,
I would play tricks all day
I'd trip people up
And then I'd run away!

Reece Hepburn (8)
Norham St Ceolwulf's CE First School, Berwick upon Tweed

Love

Love is pinky-red like roses on a summer's day,
It smells like strawberries covered in chocolate.
Love feels like fluffy bunnies,
It reminds me of my rabbit Dylan.

Ashley Fiddes (8)
Norham St Ceolwulf's CE First School, Berwick upon Tweed

If I Were . . .

If I were a teacher
I'd be the meanest in the land,
And if the kids were naughty,
I would smack them on the hand.
I'd make them eat cold custard,
And make them do hard sums.
I'd make them play in the freezing cold
And they'd go crying to their mums.

Jake Gibson (8)
Norham St Ceolwulf's CE First School, Berwick upon Tweed

A Football Match

Now the new Wembley is finally built
With loads of concrete and rubbish spilt.
Thousands came to watch the game,
And saw Man U lose in shame,
Chelsea knew they'd won the cup,
And stood on a stand to lift it up.
They held it high in the crowd,
While the fans shouted really loud.

Euan Thompson (8)
Northam St Ceolwulf's CE First School, Berwick Upon Tweed

Happiness

Happiness is green like a rainforest
with beautiful butterflies,
It sounds like monkeys swinging from vine to vine
on a summer's day.
It smells like freshly grown apples in the sun.
It looks like a boy smiling when he hugs his parents.
It feels like music to my ears,
It reminds me of beautiful times.

Josh Wilson (8)
Norham St Ceolwulf's CE First School, Berwick upon Tweed

Sadness

Sadness is purple like a stormy night,
It sounds like a tap dripping in a quiet house.
It smells like rain on a cold wet day,
It's like thunder and lightning crashing
through the sky.
It feels like being alone on a winter's day.
It reminds me of being told off.

Tammie Martin (8)
Northam St Ceolwulf's CE First School, Berwick Upon Tweed

The Ballad Of Molly The Cat

(Based on the ballad 'The Raggle Taggle Gypsies')

There once was a little cat
Who called herself fat
Her real name was Molly
And she wanted a hat

She did not have a home
Which was very sad
So she went in the shop
And was very glad

At last, she thought, *yes I'm getting a hat*
A lady walked out with a hat and a bag
I want to look like that
But I am too fat

Wait a minute, that's the hat I want
But they're all gone and there's none left
Oh no, oh no, oh no,
It's like there has been a theft.

Charlotte Wren (9)
St Joseph's RC Middle School, Hexham

The Ballad Of Lee And Jack

(Based on the ballad 'The Raggle Taggle Gypsies')

Years ago there were two friends
their names were Lee and Jack
They walked to work every day
with back-packs on their back.

In the mine one awful day, just before
their break, they heard the words,
'Run, run, run!'
There had been a big mistake.

A coal wagon reversed into the wall
and they were all killed.

Lee Davison (10)
St Joseph's RC Middle School, Hexham

The Ballad Of Old Jane

(Based on the ballad 'The Raggle Taggle Gypsies')

She is called Jane
And is very old
She gets stuck in the rain
So is very cold.

Once she needed a rest
So she had a seat at the bus stop,
She had been a begging pest
But now she's asleep in a flop.

Until along came a murderer
With a very sharp knife
Perhaps he was a burglar
But all she has got is her life.

Poor old Jane
Strewn across the floor
Who gets stuck in the rain
Cannot anymore.

Rose Kipling (10)
St Joseph's RC Middle School, Hexham

Ballad

(Based on the ballad 'The Raggle Taggle Gypsies')

Poor old Thomas was the poorest man in the country.
He walked the street.
Old Thomas was a hundred years old and kept lying down for rests.
Old Thomas stuck his head in the river and drowned and nobody
cared about poor old man Thomas.
He just laid there in the dirty old river.

Daniel Matfin (10)
St Joseph's RC Middle School, Hexham

Rob And Ben

(Based on the ballad 'The Raggle Taggle Gypsies')

This ballad is about two men,
Their names were Rob and Ben.
They been friends for a very long time,
In fact, since they were ten.

Sadly Ben and Rob went to prison,
For an awfully long long time.
They thought of a plan to get them out
But they didn't have a dime.

They dug a hole like a mole,
And arrived in the River Tyne
And found some mucky slime
But they thought they would be fine.

They had a fight in the night
And fell back in the River Tyne.
'Oh no!' they cried.
Dead, they were not so very fine.

Oliver Smith (10)
St Joseph's RC Middle School, Hexham

The Ballad Of Old Jenny

(Based on the ballad 'The Raggle Taggle Gypsies')

There was an old woman called Jenny
She grew old and sad.
A lot of people who knew her
Had always thought she was mad.

Poor old Jenny
Her life was a pest,
It made her very miserable
And she needed a lot of rest.

Poor old Jenny,
She lived in a bus stop.
All she had of her own
Were some rags, a skirt and a top.

One day she decided
Her life was a mess.
She drew out a dagger
From a belt on her dress.

She was just about to kill herself
But then stopped and hesitated,
She stopped and thought about life
Her life, she had always hated.

Her life was over
And she was dead,
Nobody cared
As Jenny bled.

Claire Frodsham (10)
St Joseph's RC Middle School, Hexham

The Ballad Of Old Tom

(Based on the ballad 'The Raggle Taggle Gypsies')

Tom was down the town begging for money,
but everybody gave a frown.
Life for Tom was never sunny
he never wore a crown.

Tom was reading a map,
he was having so much fun.
But he got caught in a trap,
he wanted to run.

Tom ran but what about the time?
The sun was going down
And there was slime
but what a relief he got there on time.

Thomas Clark (10)
St Joseph's RC Middle School, Hexham

The Ballad Of Old Stacy

(Based on the ballad 'The Raggle Taggle Gypsies')

There lived an old lady called Stacy
She laid down at night on a seat,
When young she was very lazy,
And rats came and bit at her feet.

She never got married or had fun,
So she thought that Heaven was better,
To the water she did run,
But now she was just wetter.

No one saw her, no one cares,
She cried and ran away,
She ran through fields with rabbits and hares,
And no one had time to say . . .

Dear old Stacy
Come out and play.

Molly Dixon (10)
St Joseph's RC Middle School, Hexham

Coal Mine Explosion

172 years ago at Wallsend
A big explosion killed Kim.
Bob was robbed of his job
And the death of Kim upset Jim.

Bob had a broken leg,
Jim had to look after him.
The family of Kim was very upset
And Jim missed Kim.

Bob was cross about the loss of his job,
He was cross with his boss.
His boss said, 'You are injured.'
Bob was *very cross.*

Jim went to Kim's funeral,
Jim was very sad because he felt bad.

James Bird & Ben van den Berg (10)
St Joseph's RC Middle School, Hexham

Old Jill

Old Jill sat by the dusty mill
thinking about her brothers and sisters
but mostly of Old Phil
who a man shot down with a pistol.

She was now so tired and ill
remembering her shrill scream
on the night of Old Phil's kill
and it left her alone and still.

And a beggar she became
although everyone gave her money
a beggar she would remain.
How she wished she had gone with Old Phil.

She ran over to the river
and threw herself inside
that made everyone shiver
as she floated away with the tide.

And as her heart stopped beating
she knew this was the end
she would reunite with Old Phil
and now she wouldn't have to pretend!

And whilst she was floating
some power from above
a voice came down and called her up
along with a cloud white dove.

As she walked through the clouds
she spotted a familiar figure
she called out, 'Phil, is that you?'
'Yes it's me, your speech was the trigger!'

Ellen Montgomery & Miranda Lovell (10)
St Joseph's RC Middle School, Hexham

The Tale Of Old Lilly

Lilly Bennington was very old,
She looked one hundred,
Even for one hundred she was really bold,
Everyone admired her so I am told.

Lilly Bennington walked her dog twice a day,
After that she sat down on her couch,
As she was very weak,
She heard a rumble in her stomach,
All that she could have was a tin of green leeks.

Lilly Bennington lived in an old, old house,
Not too big, not too small,
She shared her bed with many a mouse.

Sadly one day, old Lilly passed away,
Nobody knew, as nobody called,
No visitors came her way,
Whatever happened could not be foretold,
Poor old Lilly, had nothing more to say.

Loren Clarke
St Joseph's RC Middle School, Hexham

Old Nick

Old Nick was always sick
He lived in London town
Always got on people's wick
He hadn't had a nice life.

He was always sad
People walking down the street
Thought he looked bad
He didn't like the sight of friendship.

The people that were kind and nice
Walked past and said,
'Would you like a slice?'
He replied, 'Yes please.'

As he began to flop
He began to look at the view
Then he fell off the cliff top
He felt this was best.

As he went down
All the people watched him go
As he dropped to the water to drown
All the people gathered round.

Beth White & Destiny Tuck
St Joseph's RC Middle School, Hexham

Old Fred

You may remember old Fred
He was so very ill
And at his age of one hundred
He couldn't afford his pills.

He had brought some bread
But we only had one slice
To survive on for the weekend
The rest had been eaten by mice.

He was very weak
He couldn't even run
In the summer he was sweaty
His seat burnt in the sun.

He didn't have a home
In old London town
He always wore a frown
He never had a crown.

Then he got a disease
Of the latest plague which made him cough a lot
He couldn't find a doctor
Which got him in a rage and made him very hot.

So he sat down on the floor
Even though it was covered in slime
As the rats scuttled by
He then found a dime.

So he walked as far as he could
And then he saw the shop
Just a metre away from where he was
He got as far as the shop then he stopped.

He had gone out of this world
And then was put to the test
He was all in despair
Before allowed to rest.

Alasdair Kirby
St Joseph's RC Middle School, Hexham

Poor Hearts

It's a piece of cake
To drift away and let my heart break
Oh poor and rich folk
Set fire to me, watch me smoke!

Ellie Hersey (10)
St Joseph's RC Middle School, Hexham

Save The Lady

The snow dropped down around her
From high in the sky.
The lady looked upwards,
The snowflakes made her cry.

The man wanted to save her life
And all life will be well
But the lady did not want to be saved,
She was going to run away.

Callum Snowball
St Joseph's RC Middle School, Hexham

Max The Dog

Max was a lonely dog,
He saw another dog,
He walked but didn't see him,
And got a log.

Max walked and walked
Until he saw a cat.
But then kept walking until . . .
He saw a rat.

He saw a river ahead of him
But walked back.
He walked over a bridge
And . . . smack!

Max walked and stopped
And said, 'I want to go to God,'
So he did
But still was a lonely dog.

Erin Phillips (9)
St Joseph's RC Middle School, Hexham

Hurry Hamster

Lily is the owner of Hurry Hamster
She loves her lots and lots.
But sadly she passed away.
She adored playing with her pots.

Lily was very upset about the death,
But she soon forgot about it all.
She knew she would remember her,
Although she was pretty small.

Sarah Weeks (10)
St Joseph's RC Middle School, Hexham

The Mouse That Liked Cheese

There once was a tiny mouse
Who lived with a cat
The tiny mouse liked the cheese
But so did the fat cat.

The fat cat slept all day long,
The mouse, it stole the cheese
But the fat cat woke up and saw
The mouse on the cheese.

Then their was a big massive chase
It was like a big war.
The mouse tripped, it was like he skipped
And hit his head on the door.

Sam Stoves (10)
St Joseph's RC Middle School, Hexham

Mary-Kate And Snowflake

There once was an old lady,
Her name was Mary-Kate,
She lived alone in a house
And she never-ever ate.

She had a pet rabbit,
Her name was Snowflake
But she didn't last for long,
She died near a lake.

This made Mary-Kate even more sad,
The death of Snowflake,
Made her feel down
And think it was all fake.

She loved her dear Snowflake
And didn't want her to go,
She was going to buy another rabbit
But still felt very low.

Lucy Seddon (10)
St Joseph's RC Middle School, Hexham

The Silver Horse

There once was a horse
Who was beautiful, silver and gold.
All her belongings were rotting away,
Her tack was beginning to mould.

She was going to a new home,
Her owners were dying and old.
Her eyes were always sparkling,
Her new owners were outgoing and bold.

They worked her so hard,
She wept and wept.
Her old owners were now dead,
For one whole week she had not slept.

She thought of her owners, day and night,
She wanted her old hay bed.
Her owners woke one morning,
Woke to find her dead.

Beth Taylor (10)
St Joseph's RC Middle School, Hexham

The Lonely Cat

One cold night only one cat lay
Miserably, with no home.
That cat was so thin he couldn't walk,
All he could do was moan, moan, moan.

'I wish I had a home,' he said
And ran across the street.
Then everybody heard a car wheel brake,
All people could do was look at the meat.

So everybody thought that it was sad,
And that the cat was so little, everybody felt sorry for that cat
They thought they should've taken it to the vet,
But they also thought *he didn't even have a mat!*

Eleanor Donkin (9)
St Joseph's RC Middle School, Hexham

War Is A Fright

Dark was the city
Everything dull and grey
Nothing awake, no noise heard
There was nothing to say.

I walked down the street
I saw the ruined house
I heard a faint noise
Nothing was awake, not even a mouse.

I saw all the people
The bodies being carried away
The fright was now over
I was glad it was day.

It was now over
Everyone was very glad
The terrible happening was over
It was very sad.

Vincent Straub
St Joseph's RC Middle School, Hexham

The Frog

There once was a little frog
His name was Hippety Hop
He went for a little swim
Then he heard a pop.

Then he heard something coming
His heart was bumping away
He turned around and saw his mum wasn't there
But he couldn't stay.

He hopped into the river
Then he saw a dog
The dog spotted him
Then Hippety Hop was gone.

Aimee Wright (10)
St Joseph's RC Middle School, Hexham

Fizzy The Stray

Once there was a cat
He was called Fizzy,
He was very tatty,
He ran around and got dizzy.

He had an owner called David,
One day David came home very drunk
And started throwing everything around,
He looked very much like a punk.

One day he threw Fizzy out so
He went and sat in the bin,
He had no food,
All he had was a tin.

He sat around all lonely,
Sat alone he was,
He wished he had somebody,
He wished he had a friend called Roz.

He was so lonely that
He wanted to run away,
To somebody who cared,
He had nothing else to say.

So one day, he wished he could die
So he went to the river,
Looked down and saw his reflection
And jumped in cold and shivering.

Victoria Grundy
St Joseph's RC Middle School, Hexham

Tiger, Tiger

Tiger, tiger in the night
Tiger, tiger always chasing
Tiger, tiger never dirty
Tiger, tiger always racing

Tiger, tiger never in a fright
Tiger, tiger has some mould
Tiger, tiger is his name
Tiger, tiger is so old.

Tiger, tiger he will die
Tiger, tiger in his bed
Tiger, tiger he has fallen
Tiger, tiger he is dead.

Noel Wild (9)
St Joseph's RC Middle School, Hexham

The Chick With No Fur

Creak! Crack!
The chick came out,
All stubby and hairy,
He couldn't jump about.

The other eggs hatched,
All fluffy and thin,
But poor little chick,
Even thinner than a pin.

The mother bird was back,
With a fat juicy worm,
The mother bird fed
And the others would sit and learn.

But poor little chick,
He had no fame,
And said to himself,
'I haven't even got a name!'

'Away! Away!
Get out of my nest,
The chicks are asleep,
And I'm trying to get some rest!'

Down fell the chick,
A long, long way,
Like his mother had told him
He had nothing else to say.

Emma Harriet Kinrade (9)
St Joseph's RC Middle School, Hexham

My Uncle Saw A Dancing Bear

(Based on 'My Mother Saw A Dancing Bear' by Charles Causley)

Hello, my name is James
And I'm a stunt bear.
I am so sad
I miss my home.

Sometimes I cry,
I cry in front of the crowd.
I don't care,
But they care even less!

I soon will die,
I know it,
But they do and don't care.
Why is everything going black?

Stop Animal Cruelty Now!

Andrew Telfer (11)
St Joseph's RC Middle School, Hexham

How Cruel Are You?

You shouldn't be cruel to animals
You wouldn't like it to happen to you.
Animals can be our friends
Animals have feelings too.

There are many, many types of dog
Who would like to be your pet
Throw a stick in the river
They will love it and get wet.

Cats come in all sizes
And beautiful colours too.
But they can end their days in many ways
As a rug or even a shoe.

Hunters hunt and kill the bear
They do it for their skin.
They do it for the money
That must be a sin.

Sam Meleady
St Joseph's RC Middle School, Hexham

Racism

There was a boy from a far country;
It's very far from England.
He doesn't have many friends;
But he's got his brother.

Nobody really likes him
Because he's from a far, distant country,
After a while, he made a friend called Jim.
The little boy with only two friends is called Timmy.

Timmy gets chased by the down town bullies
But he out runs them every time.
Timmy can run so fast, he'll never get caught
By the down town bullies.

After a time, the bullies got what they deserved
They used to call this boy a while ago, a nerd.
The so-called nerd beat them down
And the downtown bullies could only frown.

Ryan Carr (11)
St Joseph's RC Middle School, Hexham

That Day The Bomb Went Off

As I went to work, so careless one day
I got called into my boss' office
As we talked about my pay
We heard a noise and the building shook.

We stared at each other
Then we said, 'A bomb's gone off!'
We ran to the window and what we saw was
Smoke and nails and a cough.

I felt like running
I wish I could
Where could I go?
I think I should.

What I saw
I wish I never
Cos what I saw
Will scar me forever.

So I still remember that careless day
I got called into my boss' office
That day we talked about my pay
That day the bomb went off.

Patrick Cant (10)
St Joseph's RC Middle School, Hexham

Why Argue?

Leave me alone, I can't take it,
Go just leave me shaking in this fit.
Why do you do this, hurt me so?
Are you afraid to let me go?

Be silent now and watch your tone,
I think the neighbours have heard you moan.
You must be quiet and chill out a bit,
Before I give you a proper hit.

How can I 'chill' when you threaten me,
Look at my bruises. Can't you see?
I just want to get away from here to get my life back,
Instead of sitting here and getting attacked.

Right that's it you've done it now,
You've got me going, you started a row.
Why do you do this, make me get out my fists?
I think you're ready for a real good twist.

Go away! I'll call the police
Before you make me your midnight feast
The time will come when you're locked in that cell
Then your life will be a living hell!

Lorena Armstrong Norman (11)
St Joseph's RC Middle School, Hexham

A Lonely Girl

She sits at home
and waits alone,
but still nobody comes,
she cries out loud
and sits in a pool ot tears.

She'll look out of the window
and stare and stare,
and nothing, not a soul will come.

She lies alone at night
and knuckles her face in fright,
for darkness is
all she can have.

Her mother looks after her well
but will not love,
why?
It's a mystery,
nobody can tell.

She had no father to speak of
for he died at war,
long ago,
her heart has a hole so deep
which makes life rather sore.

She sits at home alone
and waits alone
and realises,
soon enough
that life is very tough
for a lonely girl.

Phoebe Dodd
St Joseph's RC Middle School, Hexham

Racism

There once was a boy
Who was judged because of his skin.
When he sat down on a chair
He felt a sting, it was a pin.

Bullies picked him out at school,
They asked his name, he said, 'Jack.'
And they didn't hesitate
To give Jack a whack.

Everyone talked behind his back
They backed away when he asked to play.
When he arrived back at home,
He told his mum he didn't want to stay.

When he walked to school one day,
The bullies arrived, looking sly.
They pulled out some eggs and threw them,
Jack was pelted and he began to cry.

Jack was glum the next day
And the bully arrived again.
But he said, 'Sorry about all this bother,
I'd like to be friends, my name's Ken.'

Matthew McNally (10)
St Joseph's RC Middle School, Hexham

Raging Bull

I saw on that December day a proud bull, coat black and dark.
His eyes angered and tormented.
The fighter waved his sheet and danced his feet.

'Toro! Toro!' The man shouted and danced
And when the beast came, he gave a great prance.
The bull turned and gave a great stare.

The bull charged not knowing for its last time,
Head and horns going for the sheet, then suddenly
the blade was drawn.
The great beast came to a halt after its great fault.

Here now came the laughs and cheers and some
brought out the beers.
The fighter standing on his latest victim posed for pictures
in the cheers.

The only one not to move was the bull now free
of torture and misery.

Max Cooper (11)
St Joseph's RC Middle School, Hexham

Kalsie-Sooogy

(Based on 'The Jabberwocky' by Lewis Carroll)

When an awful oplysop occurred,
she didn't know what to do.
Didn't know whether to salamone or to noodle-pop.
she was stuck between a kalabiscuit.

She scrambled to the flabalosy beach
to look for fling-flang, but she couldn't get any.

Bad luck for once was on her side
and it wasn't a good time.
Kalsie-Sooogy wasn't sounding for her
last breath but near enough.

Catching shade underneath the kahanonar tree,
she sholly-wolled her way to at least try and
find some fling-flang with the prodnap she had left.
Just a tiny bit of fling-flang would keep her alive.

So she trekked into the jungle whilst trying to catch
a squid-i-squad of aloe vera from the tree.
She came along a horse-come-bleeting.

It mayello like a horse splated with a sheep,
but it was a cow.
Milk! Milk! But one thing was messed Kalsie-Sooogy
didn't like milk.

She floobed strawberry milk though
floozing her way to the doodled strawberry bush,
Kalsie-Sooogy had almost no energy left.

On her way to the sacred bush,
then all glory stood in front, for there
was the strawberry bush.

She hogy-pooged the milk and strawberries.
So she got a source of fling-flang after all.

Holly Roberts (11)
St Joseph's RC Middle School, Hexham

Rabberwocky

In the rumble, the mighty rumble
The Rabberwocky sleeps to wight
Someone yooted an earthquake
Started the Rabberwocky
Died of fright.

Liam Moss (11)
St Joseph's RC Middle School, Hexham

The Ninglepop

(Based on 'The Jabberwocky' by Lewis Carroll)

Oh how the Ninglepop it smelt
I chased poor people to Swondelpebt
Before the Ninglepop moved in
Oh how much prizes would that town win.

A burly lad named Sir McDonald
(His pa was called Sir Big MacRonald)
He set out with stuff bought straight from the gop,
To sort out the stinken Ninglepop.

He set up the spointen with shampoo and spope
And heaving himself up with a sickle rope
Eventually he reached the monsters fave
And spocked on its door. How fab, how brave.

The Ninglepop reached out and opened the door
The smell was so bad Sir McDonald fell to the floor
He reached out behind him and brought out a spuket
It was full of clean stuff like mungle and nuget.

With all his strong pike he through the full pucket
The Ninglepop screamed out with such a rucket
The sweet-smelling stuff covered him from head to wangtastic
After all of that work, the Ninglepop smelt fantastic.

Katie Frodsham
St Joseph's RC Middle School, Hexham

The Hongy Dongy Monster!

(Based on 'The Jabberwocky' by Lewis Carroll)

The Crunchbottomtastics were swooshing side to side!
His favourite food was milky flunch!
He flippityed all day!
He was a very hongy dongy monster,
Who always honged about!

He had two friends called Ballawalla and Bofy,
But they were really active!
They went to Dop World (which was a monster world).

They went to the park called Kiskics Park.
They sat under the tree and had a happy picnic!
They had milky, milky sandwiches and a Biffy milkshake!

They went to play on the swingydongy.
They went up and down, round and round,
Then they went on the slippyhongy,
Which took you upside down!

Georgina Callf
St Joseph's RC Middle School, Hexham

Jammy Snouger

(Based on 'The Jabberwocky' by Lewis Carroll)

Our town was peaceful before that Jammy Snouger,
tearing us from limb to limb came,
blood spilled all over us,
we look like cherry tomatoes.

'My son, my blacksmith,
make your finest armour,
go into the woods and follow tu tu bird
and slay that Jammy Snouger.'

When I finish it and he went into the woods,
people cheer me off into the woods,
as I enter people douding,
he will never slay that Jammy Snouger.

Looking up at the tu tu tree,
trying to find the tu tu bird,
my dad came running through and said,
'Ride my ogalybogale.'

My dad ran away as fast as the wind,
I hopped on my ogalybogale,
and grad a tanga-tastic for luck,
sud in my gud and rid along.

I big sake, 2 big sake, 3 big sake,
there is the Jammy Snouger in front of me,
and pulled out my quick-ojl, poked out his eye.
1, 2, 3, sliced his head.

Blood spalleds all over the town,
people thinking I'm dead,
tears of my family heavy like elephants
sprice, sprice, I'm alive cheers all around.

My son the king would like a word,
dear boy I give you my thanks,
so you can marry my daughter,
so he did not just get fame, he also got a girl.

Tarah Harvey
St Joseph's RC Middle School, Hexham

Daisy's Challenge

Beautiful Daisy, my chestnut mare
Relaxed and happy, without a care,
She stood in the field eating her hay
A perfect start to a perfect day.

With Bracken and Boston with Bruno and Bramble,
Up on the Fells, they'd happily ramble.
Cantering, galloping, out on the heather
Lolloping freely, friends forever.

Peace is shattered with a stallion's arrival,
He sees every pony not as friend but as a rival,
He pushes and kicks, he bucks and rears,
But the friends band together despite their fears.

By clubbing together the bullying ends,
Daisy and the stallion are soon best of friends.
They run round together, morning to night,
It's hard to believe it was the same horse that gave her a fright.

Daisy's with foal by next spring,
The foal when its born is a beautiful thing,
The stallion is proud of his beautiful horse,
And won't let him grow up a bully, of course.

Martha Jones (10)
St Joseph's RC Middle School, Hexham

The Little Old Lady

The fire is the only light
As the old lady sits
The only sound heard
Is the click of the needles as she knits.

All alone now
Her husband passed away
Her children too busy to give up time
To come and see her and stay.

Her face is lined and sad
Her days are empty and long
She never thought of the day
Everyone in her life has gone.

Gabriella Costar
St Joseph's RC Middle School, Hexham

The Nature Poem

Nature, nature, the sky is blue,
When raindrops are falling there is nothing to do.
Nature, nature, the trees are swaying,
The birds watch the children, laughing and playing.
Nature, nature when apples turn ripe,
The birds in the day, the owls in the night.
Nature, nature the baker's buns are ready,
The joggers run up the hill, slow and steady.
Nature, nature spiders and plants,
Nature, nature we give God our thanks.

Faye Williams (9)
St Robert's RC First School, Morpeth

A Food Poem For Falcons

Food, glorious food, mmm, so tasty,
Two mammoths a day,
One sloth for breakfast,
One tiger, plus two possums for lunch.
So come and have a feast tonight
And remember to sing.
A food poem for falcons

Angus Johnson (8)
St Robert's RC First School, Morpeth

I Love Nature

Butterflies in the air, it's as if they're in my tummy,
flying around with their lovely patterned wings.

Fish are in the pond, they have orange
and rainbow-coloured skin.
It's as if you are in the sky with
the sun and rainbow.

Birds are in the trees, they are singing
and tweeting and playing a beautiful song.
It's like playing a piano.
Kids are playing in the park,
it's like a herd of animals.

They are screaming and shouting very loud.
You get a headache after a while.
Insects are on the ground,
people are stamping on them,
I feel sorry for them,
they are lovely things.

Dogs and cats are fighting,
they are getting on my nerves.
The cats are miaowing and the dogs
are going *woof, woof.*
You would want them to calm down.

Anna Victoria Featherstone (8)
St Robert's RC First School, Morpeth

The Weather

W ind a cold breeze blowing through my hair
E xotic sun in the east coast of Africa
A laska's terrible avalanches fall on the people that care
T ornado sucking up everything that comes in its path
H urricane knocking things down, killing things in the Caribbean
E arthquakes shaking me through the ground
R ain splashing down like silver arrows

This is the weather around me.

Jessica Venters (9)
St Robert's RC First School, Morpeth

Sweets And Chocolate

Sweets and chocolate are yummy,
they really are so scrummy.
Chocolate is better than honey,
but hates it when it's sunny.

Sweets and chocolate are great,
that's why I use them as fishing bait.
Brussels sprouts I hate,
but chocolate and sweets are great.

I think chocolate and sweets are great,
but chocolate and sweets my mum hates.
She'd rather use them as fishing bait,
but I still think chocolate is great.

Sweets and chocolate are great,
but my mum should still hate.
Because it's trips to the dentist,
but *phew* my teeth are still great!

Louise Brett (9)
St Robert's RC First School, Morpeth

The Earth

In the night sky the stars are shimmering
In the morning the sun is shining like a sauna
The sea is swishing and swoshing about
People are roaming about
Animals are galloping and crawling
The river is as still as stone
The wind is blowing, the lake is flowing
Modern madness is going about
Monsters are scaring children
Sharks and fish are swimming in the deep blue sea
The Earth is being polluted by cars
The Earth won't last long if we do it wrong.

Charlie Hope (8)
St Robert's RC First School, Morpeth

Food And Fruit

Food is scrummy of them all
Fruit is healthy of them all
Better than honey
And it is scrummy of them all

Coke and cookies, jam and bread
Mum makes sure I'm well fed.

John Robinson (8)
St Robert's RC First School, Morpeth

All Around Me

All around me there are . . .

Flowers blooming
Blossoms looming

Birds singing
Bells ringing

Children yelling
Dustbins smelling

Babies crying
People sighing

Adults kissing
Cats hissing

High heels clomping
People chomping

Leaves are falling
The sea is calling

These are the things around me.

Emma Fisher (9)
St Robert's RC First School, Morpeth

The Sweetie Store

The sweetie store down my street
You can get tons of sweets
Lollipops, gummy snakes and scrumptious chocolate bars.

Get those pounds, bring them to the sweetie store
Get no change just *munch, munch, munch.*

Crunch, crunch, crunch
Get your teeth dug in
Crunch, crunch, crunch
Munch, munch.

Chomp, chomp, chomp
It's the best sweetie store I know.

Hannah McMahon (9)
St Robert's RC First School, Morpeth

One Except For One

All the sports are fun,
But all except for one.
Kung fu,
Someone could sneak up on you,
And shout,
'Peek-a-boo!'
But if you see me
Doing Kung fu,
I will sneak up on you,
And shout,
'Peek-a-boo!'

Luke Ackhurst (8)
St Robert's RC First School, Morpeth

Coconut

Look down there,
That's where the fun is down under me,
All the pirates out at sea,
They are all having so much fun,
Collecting gold and treasure in the sea.
Look down there under me,
That's where all the fun is.
All the mermaids on the rocks,
They are all having so much fun,
Sitting in the sun singing their mermaid song.
Look down there under me,
That's where all the fun is,
All the sea creatures under the sea
Playing and having a cup of tea,
But look at me,
I'm still stuck up in this tree.

Elspeth Cunningham (7)
St Robert's RC First School, Morpeth

Secrets

My friend told me a secret,
I really want to tell,
It's hurting in my head,
It's ringing like a bell.

I told someone a secret,
I really called it out,
But now I've told it,
I need to scream and shout.

My friend found out I told her,
She was really, really mad,
I said I was sorry,
I've been really, really bad.

My friend told me another secret,
I really want to tell,
It's hurting in my head,
It's ringing like a bell.

Lucy Havery (8)
St Robert's RC First School, Morpeth

A School Poem

School is a place to learn
and sometimes you could read a book in the playground
and you have to learn your times tables
and sometimes you get to do a science experiment
and you get to learn what the experiment's about .

Sean Shackleton-Chavez (8)
St Robert's RC First School, Morpeth

By The Glitter Sea

By the glitter sea in the sun
Where my story has just begun.
By the glitter sea in the rain
Mermaids scatter with awe and pain.
By the glitter sea in the day
Fishes come out to enjoy their play.
By the glitter sea in the morning
Sailors on their ships start yawning.
By the glitter sea in the night
Everyone will say goodnight and sleep tight.
But early in the morning when the day is dawning
Another day will begin again.

Eleanor O'Brien (8)
St Robert's RC First School, Morpeth

It's Not Fair

It's not fair Sir, when the other team score a goal,
Our goalie is eating a pear.
It's not fair Sir, when the other team score a try,
Their captain looks too sly.
It's not fair Sir, when the fielders stump us at the wicket,
Our batsman is feeding his pet cricket.

Benedict Gosling (8)
St Robert's RC First School, Morpeth

Shark

Under the sea the fish all flee,
For here comes a shark
With great white sharp teeth.
A swish of his tail,
The fish all scatter and you can hear the chatter.
But here comes a bigger killer whale,
The whale saves the fish but can he save himself!

Esmee Webley (8)
St Robert's RC First School, Morpeth

Island

Here is the island
In the sun
Pirates fighting
Mermaids singing in the sea.

Jonathon Carlile (8)
St Robert's RC First School, Morpeth

The Sea

See a shark in the deep
Dolphins squeak goodbye
Shipwrecks in the blue
Mermaids and their sparkling tails
Treasure ahoy!
Jellyfish and their stinging legs
Water crashing rocks
Wind like steel
Whales eating ships
That's my ship's bait.

Megan McMahon (7)
St Robert's RC First School, Morpeth

Who Am I?

I'm as fast as a car
In lots of different countries
I last for hours
I need fuel
Sometimes I have steam
I am long and sometimes short
I leave at my port
I have a loyal driver
Who drives round the track
Come and tell me what I am
But make sure you don't crack.

Who am I?

Emily Todd (8)
St Robert's RC First School, Morpeth

Island In The Sun

I'm a pirate looking for treasure, mermaids or even a feather
I go past glistening sands
I'm a pirate looking for gold
Watch out for jellyfish, they might have a sting
Everything I see I want to have
Except for those nasty shipwrecks with battered sails
and broken rails.

Daniel Almond (7)
St Robert's RC First School, Morpeth

My Island

Here's my island out in the sea
Under the sun where mermaids are singing
Like a bell ringing on top of the glistening sands
I see the pirates sailing their ships
I hear the waves crashing against the shore
I listen to the dolphins squeaking more and more
Whales and dolphins and fish in the sea
This is what makes the island so fun
This is the island under the sun - so, so fun.

Emma Shuttleworth (8)
St Robert's RC First School, Morpeth

Star Light

I went to bed one night looking at the stars
Twinkling up high, oh what a pretty sight
Stars sparkling up high.

I went to bed one night looking at the stars
Glowing above me
Oh what a pretty sight it was
I went to bed one night.

Alex Mould (9)
St Robert's RC First School, Morpeth

In My Back Garden

In my back garden
I have a hose
I do use it
But not up my nose.

In my back garden
I have a gnome
And every time I go there
It has a good poem.

In my back garden
I have a mouse
But sometimes
It goes into the house.

In my back garden
I have a pool
Then after I swim in it
I go to school.

In my back garden
I have a dog
It always
Chews on a great big log.

In my back garden
I always make
Guess what it is
It's a use of a rake.

In my back garden
I have a flower
And it has
A secret power.

James Currie (9)
St Robert's RC First School, Morpeth

I Remember

Looking at the beach in the hot sun,
Looking at my dog shake water off his coat,
Looking at my dogs for nothing.

The taste of my dogs' wet fur, yuck!
Tasting salty water on a hot day.

Smelling my half sister's clothes in the sun,
Smelling hot water in the cold winter.

Touching my dogs' fur, nice and warm,
Touching my dad's coat, soft as feathers.

Hearing my two dogs bark at birds, what a pity,
Hearing my ferret play at night.

Kayleigh Brown (9)
Sedbergh Primary School, Sedbergh

My Farm

Looking at the lambs jumping in the field,
Looking at my dog prancing around in the field,
rounding up the sheep,
Looking at the lambs suckling on their mothers.

Smelling the sweet hay in the field,
Smelling the dip in the dipping tub,
Smelling the roast lamb when I'm walking to the house door.

Touching the lambs that are wet and slimy,
that have just come out of their mothers,
Touching my dog's soft fur on a winter's morning,
Touching the hard horns that have fallen from the sheep.

Hearing the sizzling of pork sausages in the pan,
Hearing the hungry sheep bleating in the morning,
Hearing my dad's battered pick-up coming up the lane.

Tasting the pork sausage in my mouth,
Tasting roast lamb for my Sunday dinner,
Tasting my cornflakes in the morning.

Emma Dawson (9)
Sedbergh Primary School, Sedbergh

My Farm

Looking at the lambs just been born,
Looking at the cows jumping in the field,
Looking at the hens flying in the wind.

Smelling the fresh hay just been made,
Smelling the dipping tub in the sheep pens,
Smelling the silo in the building.

Touching the cuddly lambs, stroking them gently,
Touching the calves very delicately,
Touching the hay, it is very prickly,
Touching the hens' eggs nice and warm.

Hearing the lambs bleating in the shed,
Hearing the cows mooing in the field,
Hearing hens clucking in the yard,
Hearing the dogs barking in their bed.

Tasting the lamb with mint sauce,
Tasting the beef with gravy,
Tasting the hen eggs, nice and yellow.

Leanne Postlethwaite (9)
Sedbergh Primary School, Sedbergh

My Holiday

Looking at the waves on the seaside,
Looking at all the seagulls flying about in the wind,
Looking at the hotel where I go to sleep.

Tasting the bacon every morning for my breakfast,
Tasting the pudding that has just come out of the oven,
Tasting the lovely food from the bar.

Touching all the dry sand on my feet,
Touching the cold wet sea on my fingers,
Touching my cosy bed when I go to sleep at night.

Smelling the tasty fry-up for my breakfast,
Smelling that holiday smell,
Smelling the hotel room when I come home at night.

Hearing all the seagulls waking me up,
Hearing all the traffic from the motorway,
Hearing the engine of my car on my way home.

Chloe Kendal (9)
Sedbergh Primary School, Sedbergh

I Remember My Holiday

Looking out of the window of the hotel room
Looking at my mum coming back from the pool
Looking at the trains setting off from the station.

Tasting the sweet and sour at the bar
Tasting the after pudding of the chocolate sauce
Tasting the orange juice with the umbrella.

Smelling the soap of the people in the shower room
Smelling the paint in the art room
Smelling the fresh air of the outdoor wood.

Touching the sand on the beach
Touching the smooth bedcover in my room
Touching the smooth back of the dog.

Hearing the people laughing in the pub
Hearing the birds chirping in the morning
Hearing the sound of the waterfall.

Erin Hoggarth Raw (9)
Sedbergh Primary School, Sedbergh

My Thoughts

Tasting the rich toffee in sticky toffee pudding,
Tasting the oaty nuts in crunchy nut clusters,
Tasting my mum's mean apple crumble.

Looking at the pizza melting in the oven,
Looking at the cabbage being chopped in half with a machete,
Looking at the apples being picked off the tree and made
into apple crumble.

Hearing the beef spit in the oven,
Hearing the apples fall off the trees,
Hearing the kettle boil on a cold day.

Smelling the fresh bread out of the oven,
Smelling the nice apple in your mouth,
Smelling the stew in the saucepan.

John Woof (9)
Sedbergh Primary School, Sedbergh

On The Farm

Listening to the tractor on a summer morning,
Listening to the till rattling out of the bottom of the till spreader.

Smelling the hay on a hot summer's day,
Smelling the bacon on a winter's morning.

Tasting the hot soup on a morning,
Tasting the milk in my hot tea.

Looking at the lambs eating their food,
Looking at Dad doing something on the tractor.

William Dawson (9)
Sedbergh Primary School, Sedbergh

My Family

Looking at my family altogether, smiling, laughing in all weather,
Looking at my ancestors' faces,
Looking at my mum and dad smiling at each other.

Tasting my dad's lasagne,
Tasting my mum's black beans and rice.

Smelling Mum's clothes and blankets,
Smelling freshly made food.

Hearing my dad coming home from work,
Touching my sister's silky hair.

Charlotte Young Andrade (9)
Sedbergh Primary School, Sedbergh

I Remember

Listening to the birds at the seaside when I wake up
in the camper van.
Listening to the long grass at Siloth swaying in the breeze.

Touching the sand and letting it run through my hand,
Touching the smooth worn-down glass.

Smelling the salty breeze in the morning,
Smelling the bacon and egg buttie in the shop.

Tasting the double scoop ice cream,
Tasting the bacon and egg buttie with butter running down my chin.

Looking at the seagulls flying over the camper van through the window,
Looking at the waves splashing against the rocks and on my shirt.

Sam Fearnhead (9)
Sedbergh Primary School, Sedbergh

I Remember

I remember . . .
Smelling my dog in the winter
Looking at his gleaming eyes in the sunlight,
Listening to him do a sudden growl after barking,
Touching his soft warm fur.

I remember . . .
The look of my cat's smile when I stroke her,
Smelling her fur as she lies quietly on the sofa,
Feeling her fur as soft as cotton.

I remember . . .
The smile on my friend's face,
His gleaming gold hair thrusting the air as he runs,
His big blue glowing eyes in the sun,
His bright face when he's happy.

That's what I remember.

Terence Glanville (9)
Sedbergh Primary School, Sedbergh

My Tea

I can see sausages sizzling in the pan, almost ready to eat
I can taste ice cream freezing like the top of a mountain
I can hear popcorn popping in a pan
I can smell the chocolate pudding being cooked on the stove
I can feel a smooth red apple rolling in my hands
I can see an orange which is very juicy
I can taste the sour taste of lemon in my mouth
I can hear the sound of a pancake falling after a flight in the air
I can smell the smell of bacon roasting good and proper
I can feel a banana curved and tasty
I can see a table set for my tea - yum-yum.

Miles Blanch (9)
Sedbergh Primary School, Sedbergh

Going To Sleep

Looking at the ceiling and finding pictures in the wallpaper,
Tasting the taste of Teddy's ear as I suck it slowly whilst drifting off,
Smelling the lovely smell of my pillow when it's just been washed,
Feeling the worn cover of my duvet that keeps me warm each night,
Hearing the occasional car as it trundles past our house.

Thomas Hinson (9)
Sedbergh Primary School, Sedbergh

I Remember

I remember . . .
Looking at the sea in Morecambe,
Looking at the Statue of Liberty in America.

I remember . . .
Tasting McDonald's crunchy instant apple pie,
Tasting sweet Super Noodles from ASDA,
Tasting my mum's fat home-made chips.

I remember . . .
Touching the plastic on the window frame,
Touching my cool TARDIS play set.

I remember . . .
Smelling the flavour of the best rice in the world.

I remember . . .
Hearing my mum slamming the broken, crooked door.

Luke Robinson (9)
Sedbergh Primary School, Sedbergh

My Family

Looking at the grin on my mum's face,
Looking at my half brother's guitar,
Looking at my dad playing the piano, sticking out his tongue to help him concentrate.

Tasting my grandma's apple crumble,
Tasting my dad's meaty spaghetti Bolognese,
Tasting my auntie's sticky toffee pudding.

Smelling the mothbally smell of my grandma who's long gone,
Smelling my baby cousin's freshly washed clothes,
Smelling my mum's best perfume.

Touching my cousin's long blonde hair,
Touching my mum's dangly emerald earrings,
Touching my grandma's fleecy warm coat.

Listening to my twin brother playing on his PS2,
Listening to my mum's singing, whilst she's cooking tea,
Listening to my whole family's unique voices.

Francine Glanville (9)
Sedbergh Primary School, Sedbergh

My Dog

Looking at his black fur,
Looking for him when he is swimming,
Looking for him when we take him on a walk,
Looking for him when he chases a cat.

Touching his wet soggy nose,
Touching his soft fur before I go to bed,
Touching his soft pad on his foot,
Touching his soft tail when it hits me.

Hearing his bark to tell you someone is there,
Hearing him play happily in the garden,
Hearing him splash into the water,
Hearing him scratch across the floor.

Smelling the smell of his wet fur,
Smelling his food - it smells disgusting,
Smelling his shampoo, it's deadly,
Smelling his bed in the living room.

Hannah Stephenson (9)
Sedbergh Primary School, Sedbergh

My Holiday

Hearing the sound of the rain hitting my window at night,
Hearing the sound of the Indians playing their music in Portugal,
Hearing the sound of the bell ringing when the food is ready in the beach bar.

Tasting the meat kebab on the hot night in Lagos,
Tasting the hot bread straight from the Portuguese shop,
Tasting the cool juice on the aeroplane.

Looking at the Indians dancing in the streets,
Looking at the statues in Lagos Centre,
Looking at the waves crashing on the beach on a hot sunny day.

Touching the red-hot sand on the beautiful beach,
Touching the ice-cold lolly juice running down my fingers,
Touching the runny water falling through my fingers
in my swimming pool.

Smelling the lovely hot air when I step off the plane,
Smelling the Chinese food when Dad and me go and pick it up,
Smelling the hot bread and meat in the supermarket,
Smelling the ice cream running down my arm.

That's my holiday.

Liam Ball (9)
Sedbergh Primary School, Sedbergh

My Farm

Looking at the cows getting fatter every day,
Looking at the lambs getting bigger every hour,
Looking at the hens lying in the hut.

Smelling the juicy silo early in the morning,
Smelling the muck on the fields from yesterday,
Smelling the oil dripping off the old David Brown.

Tasting the free range eggs fresh from the hut,
Tasting the fresh ripe potatoes from the fields,
Tasting the fat cows in the shed.

Nathan Handley (9)
Sedbergh Primary School, Sedbergh

My Home

I like the smell of my mum's cleaning liquid
when she's been tidying my bedroom.
I like the smell of my mum's cooking on a Sunday.
I like the sound of sizzling chips.
I like the sound of my mum, happily asking me
if I've had a good day at school.
Tasting nice warm soup on a Saturday night.
Tasting chicken in batter with gravy on top.
Touching my nice soft bed and lying on it.
Touching my dog's soft fur when I get home.

I remember hearing my dad's car when he comes back from work.

Jake Cowperthwaite (9)
Sedbergh Primary School, Sedbergh

Dreams

I opened my closet and out popped a dream,
It wasn't heavy 'cause it didn't lean.
But it jumped around hand to hand,
And sliding along like jelly-like sand.
It danced down the stairs and buttered some toast,
It was really quite spooky, I suppose like a ghost.
It pulled out the laptop and guess what it did?
It went on the Internet and played like a kid.
Then it went in the garden and on the trampoline,
It could do forward rolls and flips, it was really quite amazing.
Then to my surprise it went back in the kitchen
and ate its buttered toast,
(It must have been famished)
And then in one jiffy it just vanished!

Willa Elliot (8)
Tweedmouth West First School, Berwick upon Tweed

The Cheetah

Timid and shy
Powerful and fast
Hiding in the tallest grass
Tiny ears, amber eyes
In the sun the cheetah lies
When the cheetah
Senses danger
He prepares to fight the stranger
When the cheetah eats his prey
The lions and leopards
Take it away
Then the cheetah has no food
Because the lion and leopards
Were so rude
So please understand the cheetah's plight
For if you shoot it, it won't be right
So don't let the cheetah become extinct
It's the most beautiful animal on Earth
I think.

Keegan Gillam (8)
Tweedmouth West First School, Berwick upon Tweed

Bears

Watch out
because you
will get a scare
if you see
a bear.
It's brown
and creepy
but has claws
that are freaky.
They are
very big
and they
love to dig.
Bears live
in the wood
and eat food
like leaves and foxes.
So have
a lot of care
because you might
see a bear!

Emily Robinson (8)
Tweedmouth West First School, Berwick upon Tweed

Spiders

Spiders are horrible
And very gooey
They can be tiny
But if you eat
Them I think
They will be
Very chewy
Spiders are crawly
Creepy and freaky
And might crawl
Into your mouth
When you yawn
Because you are sleepy
So that is the story
Of the creepy and
Sneaky spiders
So watch out
They might be
Hidden behind your
Finders.

Katie Boyd (8)
Tweedmouth West First School, Berwick upon Tweed

School

I went to my school one day
And what did the teacher say?
'You have been too naughty to go out and play,
So you will have to do detention all day.'

Sophie Akers (9)
Tweedmouth West First School, Berwick upon Tweed

The Space Adventure

My space adventure away up high,
Even above the great big sky.
All the stars swooshing past,
Are we there at last?
Now we have landed on the planet Mars,
I can't believe there are no cars.
Now it's time to go way
I'll have many things to say,
Like I've been in a rocket
Bigger than a giant's pocket.
I've been to space
A different place,
That's my space adventure.

Fraser Young (8)
Tweedmouth West First School, Berwick upon Tweed

Monsters

Monsters can be big and tall,
Monsters can be tiny and small.
Some are dark green,
Some are mega mean.
They are fat,
They have ears like a cat.
Also smelly,
Also wear wellies.
They can be the size of a gnat
And that is that.

Gabriel Freeman (7)
Tweedmouth West First School, Berwick upon Tweed

Moon, Moon

Moon, Moon go away far,
Moon, Moon sing to the star.
Moon, Moon what have you done?
Moon, Moon we will have lots of fun.
Moon, Moon carry me there,
Moon, Moon let's play at the fair.
Moon, Moon take me to my bear,
Moon, Moon help me say my prayer.

Annie Heath (8)
Tweedmouth West First School, Berwick upon Tweed

Friendship

With me
And my friends
The fun never ends
And if you want to know their names
You will have to join in our games
There's Fae and Emma
And Bethany and Gemma
I hope you'll join us in the end
And with it you'll have a friend.

Lauren Park (9)
Tweedmouth West First School, Berwick pon Tweed

Friends

Friends, friends, I have so many of them
I will name them on my fingers
There's Melissa, Emily, Annie, Zoe, Gemma, Mandy and Charley
I told you so, I have so much fun with them
We play different games every day
So come and join in the fun.

Katrina Macdermid (8)
Tweedmouth West First School, Berwick upon Tweed

Rabbits

Rabbits can be white, brown and black
They thump with their feet at the back
Rabbits come in different breeds
I love the ones who always feed
Even when it tires out
I love that one without a doubt.

Melissa Mee (9)
Tweedmouth West First School, Berwick upon Tweed

Hamsters

Furry hamsters love to play,
They play and play every day.
Even when the sun is shining,
All these hamsters are still smiling.
They love their wheels and they run till it's done.
Even when it's time for bed,
They never get that in their heads.
They're always up for a snack or two,
But they always live in the blues.

Gemma Hutchinson (9)
Tweedmouth West First School, Berwick upon Tweed

Army

Army is scary
It makes you feel weary
The bangs and bangs
Coming towards you
When you do not know what to do
Because you're standing on the spot
And your belly's in a knot.

Tom McLeod (9)
Tweedmouth West First School, Berwick upon Tweed

Dinosaurs

Dinosaurs can be tall
Dinosaurs can be small
Dinosaurs can be flat
Dinosaurs can be fat
Dinosaurs can be dumb
Dinosaurs can be fun
Dinosaurs can be tough
Dinosaurs can be rough.

Emma Johnston (9)
Tweedmouth West First School, Berwick upon Tweed

Fish

Fish can be small
and big and tall
Fish can be flat
and bigger than a cat
Fish can be orange, blue and white
Fish can be very bright.

Rachel May Simpson (8)
Tweedmouth West First School, Berwick upon Tweed

Pets

What animals do I like?
I like . . .
Bunnies, guinea pigs and dogs
Hamsters, cows and sheep
I know it is fun
So I am ready to run
Away with my new pet
But I think I need another pet
What should I get?
A pig, a duck or maybe a lion
I want them all.

Zoe Tait (9)
Tweedmouth West First School, Berwick upon Tweed

Teddy Bears

Teddy bears love to play
They play a lot almost every day
Teddy bears what are their names
Brown Ted, Pretty Princess and even James
Teddy bears, what are their games?
Hide-and-seek, beary brains
Guess who? and what daisy chains.
Teddy bears, what do they like?
They like to go to bed at night.

Sian Hush (8)
Tweedmouth West First School, Berwick upon Tweed

Teddy Bears

Five, ten or maybe twenty
I have brown ones, I have blue
Don't forget the green ones too
Fuzzy ears and shiny eyes
Like two glistening suns in the skies
Dark bright, tall or tiny
There's just so many
Smart, dumb or even in-between
Molly, Tina, Tom or Jack
Doesn't matter what they're called
They're my teddy bears.

Iona Frame (9)
Tweedmouth West First School, Berwick upon Tweed

Dogs, Dogs, Dogs

Dogs, dogs, dogs
Dancing in clogs
Dogs, dogs, dogs
Dipping in bog

Dogs, dogs, dogs
Slipping on ice
Dogs, dogs, dogs
Chasing mice

Dogs, dogs, dogs
Going to the park
Dogs, dogs, dogs
It's getting dark.

Ellie Hogarty (9)
Tweedmouth West First School, Berwick upon Tweed

Young Writers Information

We hope you have enjoyed reading this book - and that you will continue to enjoy it in the coming years.

If you like reading and writing poetry drop us a line, or give us a call, and we'll send you a free information pack.

Alternatively if you would like to order further copies of this book or any of our other titles, then please give us a call or log onto our website at www.youngwriters.co.uk

Young Writers Information
Remus House
Coltsfoot Drive
Peterborough
PE2 9JX

(01733) 890066